Our Lady of Fatima

Our Mother Comes To Us

"Pray, pray a great deal and make sacrifices for sinners, for many souls go to hell because they have no one to pray and make sacrifices for them."
—Our Lady of Fatima

International Pilgrim Virgin Statue Foundation, Inc.
Munster, IN 46321

IMPRIMATUR: † Most Rev. Dale J. Melczek
Bishop of Gary, Indiana

FATIMA PORTUGAL 1917

As you already know, the Mother of Jesus, the Most Holy Virgin Mary, appeared to three children at Fatima, Portugal during the summer of 1917. Beginning on May 13th and again on the 13th of each month until October 13th, Mary gave the world a message called the "Peace Plan from Heaven"; calling us to conversion, prayer, and penance. "If what I tell you is done, many sinners will be converted and there will be peace." "... Pray, pray a great deal and make sacrifices for sinners, for many souls go to hell because they have no one to pray and make sacrifices for them."

On July 13th the Virgin promised a great miracle on October 13th "so that all may believe." The great miracle of the sun occurred as foretold on that day with about 100,000 people gathered at Fatima witnessing it, including atheist newspaper reporters who acknowledged it as a miracle in the Portuguese press.

The Message of July 13th also warned that by failing to do as she asks; we will suffer from "wars, famine and persecution of the church." "The good will be martyred; the Holy Father will have much to suffer; and various nations will be annihilated. Finally, my Immaculate Heart will triumph, and a period of peace will be granted to the world."

On May 13, 2000, Pope John Paul II declared

1

two of the three children "Blessed," during a ceremony at Fatima attended by hundreds of thousands.[1] He spoke of the urgency of the message in the new millennium and said it places a "burden on the church" because of its gospel call to reparation.

INTERNATIONAL PILGRIM VIRGIN STATUE OF OUR LADY OF FATIMA

Realizing that most of the world's people were not hearing about the Fatima Message, it was decided to send a statue on a teaching mission. Since 1947 the Pilgrim Statue has been traveling across the world bringing the presence of Mary and Her message. Miracles of conversion and cures have occurred along the way.

Pope Pius XII, in his radio message to the pilgrims at Fatima, May 13, 1951, reflected on Mary as Queen of the World and remarked that the Pilgrim Statue goes forth traveling as though to claim her dominion, "and the favors She performs along the way are such that we can hardly believe what we are seeing with our eyes."

An official documentarian of Fatima said: "Never in the history of the Church have charismas descended in such abundance on the people of God as through the Pilgrim Virgin."[2]

---

1. The third child, Lucia, died on February 13, 2005.

2. The Rev. Dr. Joaquim Alonso.

What is astounding is the fact that, even in countries with a minority of Catholics, millions of people gathered for visits of this Holy Statue.

Miracle of Tears

The Bishop of Fatima himself three times accompanied this Pilgrim Virgin Statue around the entire world. On more than 30 occasions it is reported to have shed human tears. Photographs of the statue weeping appeared in newspapers around the world.

Over 100 million pictures of the statue, in full color, have been distributed in more than 50 countries, in various languages, on a leaflet with the title: *Look Into Her Eyes,* calling people to respond to the Message of Fatima.

The leaflet explains that these are the eyes of a statue, but not just of ANY statue. These are the eyes of the International Pilgrim Virgin which have shed tears as She traveled the world "to claim Her dominion."

Many say that it seems to be truly Our Lady Herself who has gone forth to remind Her children of the conditions which must be met before we can have the triumph She has promised.

Our Commitment is Needed Now!

In a special letter to the Bishop of Fatima, issued on October 13, 1997, Pope John Paul II said: *"On the threshold of the third millennium, as we observe the signs of the times of this 2Oth century, Fatima is certainly one of the greatest."*

The Holy Father then points out that in this great *sign we are presented with an alternative: war or peace.* He says one of the main reasons Fatima is one of the greatest signs of these times is *"because its message announces many of the later events and conditions them on the response to its appeals."*

We will not have the promise without the response. And Our Lady seems to be traveling the world to evoke our response.

Indeed, the visit of the Pilgrim Virgin Statue to you brings a special responsibility. As the Holy Father has said, the triumph depends on OUR response. And if we have had Our Lady's visit do we not have a special obligation to respond?

After some 25 million persons around the world responded by making the basic pledge (found on page 27 of this leaflet), we had the dissolution of the Soviet Union.

Also, in that October 1997 letter, the Pope said that She is anxious *"to save mankind from self-destruction."* And, he also said that, *"in Our Lady of Fatima, God is now giving a refuge to the world: the refuge of Her Immaculate Heart."*

Purpose of the Pilgrim Virgin Statue

At each visit, in dioceses and parishes, the statue is the occasion for a renewal of consecration to Her Immaculate Heart as the statue is crowned in recognition of Her Queenship. This follows the spirit and the mandate of the encyclical of Pope Pius XII on the Queenship of Mary.

The encyclical says: "in this doctrine and devotion of Our Lady's Queenship lies the world's greatest hope" and refers to the statue of Our Lady of Fatima as the *"the messenger of Her royalty."* It requires that each year on the feast of Our Lady's Queenship *"there be renewed consecration to Her Immaculate Heart."*

Like that Feast Day, these visits of the Pilgrim Virgin around the world provide special occasions for the renewal of consecration to Her Immaculate Heart and to the Eucharistic Heart of Jesus in response to Her Fatima message.

The Third Secret Revealed

Part of the July 13, 1917 message from Our Lady was not made public at the time and was called "The Third Secret of Fatima." On May 13, 2000, Pope John Paul II announced that he had given orders for the secret to be revealed with a commentary. It was made public on June 26, 2000. It consists of two prophetic visions.

In the first vision Lucia writes, "At the left of Our Lady and a little above, we saw an Angel with a flaming sword in his left hand; flashing, it gave out flames that looked as though they would set the world on fire. But, they died out in contact with the splendor that Our Lady radiated towards him from Her right hand. Pointing to the earth with his right hand, the Angel cried out in a loud voice: "Penance, Penance, Penance!"

In the second vision "We saw, in an immense light that is God (something similar to how people appear in a mirror when they pass in front of it), a Bishop dressed in white (we had the impression it was the Holy Father). Other bishops, priests, men and women religious, going up a steep mountain, at the top of which was a big Cross of rough-hewn trunks as of a cork tree with bark."

"Before reaching there, the Holy Father passed through a big city half in ruins. And half trembling with halting step, afflicted with pain and sorrow, he prayed for the souls of the corpses he met on his way."

"Having reached the top of the mountain, on his knees at the foot of the big Cross, he was killed by a group of soldiers who fired bullets and arrows at him. And in the same way, there died, one after another, the other bishops, priests, men and women religious, and various lay people of different ranks and positions."

"Beneath the two arms of the Cross there were two Angels, each with a crystal aspersorium in his hand, in which they gathered up the blood of the Martyrs and with it sprinkled the souls that were making their way to God."

Before releasing this last secret of Fatima, Pope John Paul II asked Sister Lucia (who received this secret from Our Lady of Fatima in *1917) for her interpretation.* She replied that the visions (of the Angel of Justice, the mountain of corpses, the ruined city, etc.) referred to the part of Our Lady's message, which ended with the words *"several entire nations will be annihilated."*

She added: *"If we have not yet seen the complete fulfillment of the final part of this prophecy, we are going toward it little by little with great strides."*

The urgency of our response becomes evident in the fact that the Holy Father decided to make the secret known in June 2000, and in his words: She seemed to indicate that *the world is almost inexorably proceeding to self-destruction.* The Pope seemed to share this view in his Fatima letter of October 13, 1997, in which His Holiness said the greatness of Fatima is that it gives the specific formula *"to save mankind from self-destruction."*

"As we approach the new millennium it seems that the words of Our Lady of Fatima *are nearing their fulfillment."*

Deadline

SO FAR, with the help of a few generous souls, the Mother of Jesus has been holding back the Angel's strike. But according to Sister Lucia, it seems we are nearing a deadline after which it could be too late.

Now the secret has been revealed *while it is still NOT too late!*

As already mentioned, Pope Pius XII said that

through the Pilgrim Virgin, with Her miracles and tears, Our Lady Herself seems to have gone forth to "claim Her dominion." She comes to you to ask you to help Her not only hold back the sword of Divine Justice, but to prevent it from striking.

In Her first words of the July apparition (the apparition of the secret), Our Blessed Mother said "Pray the rosary every day in honor of Our Lady of the Rosary in order to obtain peace for the world and the end of the war, because only She can help you."

We find an excellent example of this in the Bible. God entrusted the deliverance of His people to Moses as He now entrusts our deliverance to Our Heavenly Mother. (Exodus 17:9-15)

Holding Up the Arms of Moses

Moses prayed with outstretched arms when the battle was going badly for the Israelites against the forces of Amalec. As long as he did so the battle went in the favor of God's people. When Moses could no longer hold out his arms, the battle favored the forces of Amalec.

The holy followers of Moses *held up his arms until the victory was won.*

This is what we must do for Our Lady, to whom, as Blessed Jacinta said, God has now *"entrusted the peace of the world"* as He once entrusted victory to Moses.

Needed now are a *sufficient* number to respond to Her call.

St. Padre Pio indicated this when he said, ***"Russia will be converted when there is a Fatima Apostle for every Communist.'"*** (You become a Fatima Apostle when you make the pledge on page 27 of this booklet.)

This modern Saint and prophet was saying: ***"The victory will come*** when there are a ***sufficient number*** responding to Our Lady's requests."

In the light of the revelation of the final secret of Fatima, that need of a sufficient number is reaching a deadline. The Vatican document explaining the Third Secret makes this very clear: *"The Angel with the flaming sword"* recalls similar images in the Book of Revelation. This represents the threat of judgment over the world. Today the prospect that the world might be reduced to ashes by a sea of fire is no longer pure fantasy. Man, himself, with his inventions, has forged the flaming sword.

Will we obtain the sufficient number in time to prevent that flaming sword from striking us?

Respond to Her call! Respond to Her tears! Make the pledge at the end of this booklet today!

In the Third Secret of Fatima, it is revealed that Our Lady of Fatima has been able to hold back the fiery sword of God's justice until now, while the cry of the Angel resounds over the Earth with the words: ***"PENANCE, PENANCE, PENANCE"***

Is it now time for the whole world to awaken at last to this Message given by Our Lady of

Fatima in 1917, a Message telling us that if we continue to refuse to listen, *"SEVERAL ENTIRE NATIONS WILL BE ANNIHILATED"!*

As Pope John Paul II has said over and over, response to the requests of **Our Lady of Fatima is more urgent than ever.**

Look Into Her Eyes

This is the message which the Pilgrim Virgin, having traveled the world since 1947 as an anxious mother, brings to us.

You look at the statue. There are no words. But there is an experience of Her presence. Looking into the eyes one remembers that more than thirty times they shed tears before many witnesses. It is as though looking into the eyes of your mother.

Her glance seems mixed with sadness and concern. She is an anxious mother who comes ... to use the very words of the recent letter of Pope John Paul II: *"To save mankind from self-destruction . . ."* And the Pope added: *"Beneath Her maternal mantle, which extends from Fatima over the whole world, humanity senses anew it's longing for the Father's house and for His Bread."* (cf. Lk. 15:17).

Since Our Lady brought us the experience of Her presence without speaking, how can we know Her message? How can we know the response She is seeking so anxiously **"to save man from himself"** as the Holy Father said in that recent letter?

A Few Can Make the Difference

At the close of his recent letter (Oct. 13, 1997) for the 80th anniversary of the Fatima Miracle the Pope said:

"The salvation of many depends on the prayers and voluntary mortifications of the members of the Mystical Body of Christ... on the cooperation of pastors and faithful... particularly the prayers of families..."

The Holy Father reminds us that the response of a few can make a great difference. Indeed, you... joined to the more than 25 million around the world who have pledged to fulfill Our Lady's requests... may be the last person needed to give fruit to that great hope as we enter the third millennium: **"the hope of the definitive coming of the kingdom."**

Turn again to the front of this booklet. Look into Her eyes. Say "Yes" to Her as She said "Yes" for you over 2,000 years ago! And share this, "One of the greatest signs of our times," with others! **This is a request of our Mother of Heaven to you! What will be your answer?**

First Request of Our Mother: Three Things to be Done

Asked what was absolutely necessary for the triumph announced at Fatima, Sister Lucia, who received the messages of Our Lady of Fatima, said there were three things to be done:

1) Sanctification of daily duties
   (the morning offering)
2) Prayer (the daily Rosary)
3) Consecration to the Immaculate Heart
   of Mary (the Scapular)

These three conditions were formulated with Sister Lucia into a "Pledge" which the Bishop of Fatima authorized to be promoted as the authentic message of Fatima. More than 25 million Catholics around the world have made this basic pledge.

Second Request of Our Mother: The First Saturday Devotion

During her third apparition, on July 13, 1917, the Blessed Virgin announced that she would come again to ask for "... the Communion of reparation on the first Saturdays." Thus, on December 10, 1925, the Blessed Virgin, with the Child Jesus at her side, appeared to Lucia saying: "My daughter, look at my Heart surrounded with the thorns with which ungrateful men pierce me constantly through blasphemies and ingratitude. You, at least, try to console me, and tell people that I promise to assist at the hour of death with all the graces necessary for salvation all those who, on the first Saturday of five consecutive months:

• Confession, (the confession can be made eight days and even more, before or after the first Saturday).
• Receive Holy Communion
• Pray five decades of the Rosary

- And keep me company for 15 minutes meditating on one or more of the mysteries with the intention of offering me reparation.

With this second pledge we are asked that, if First Friday/First Saturday celebrations are held in our parish, we will consider participating as an act of consolation to the Sacred Heart of Jesus and the Immaculate Heart of Mary.

Two Pledges—Three Promises

Now we can expect the promised triumph of the Immaculate Heart of Mary with "an era of peace for mankind" if ALL the requests of Our Lady are fulfilled by enough of us.

As a personal incentive, Our Lady has made two other great promises attached to the fulfillment of these two pledges. The first pledge, with enrollment in the Scapular by a priest and wearing it perseveringly, **gives assurance of salvation and liberation from Purgatory soon after death (usually understood to mean the First Saturday).**

Attached to the second pledge is Our Lady's promise: "I promise to assist at the hour of death with all the graces necessary."

The Basic Pledge

I pledge to say five decades of the Rosary daily, to say the morning offering, and to wear the Scapular of Mt. Carmel as a sign of consecration to the Immaculate Heart of Mary.

I request by this pledge to be eligible for the Sabbatine Privilege, to have my name taken to Fatima to be buried near the site of the apparitions, and to share with the millions of others throughout the world who have made this pledge.

The First Saturday Pledge

Responding to the words of Our Lady of Fatima who said "To prevent this (i.e. that various nations will be annihilated) I shall come to ask for Communions of reparation on the first Saturday of the month." I hereby pledge, in reparation to the Immaculate Heart of Mary, to go to Confession and Communion, to say the Rosary, and to spend fifteen minutes meditating on the mysteries of the Rosary on five consecutive first Saturdays.

I will also be open to first Friday-Saturday vigils, and to receiving Communion often in reparation to the Eucharistic Heart of Jesus and the Immaculate Heart of Mary.

Use the slip found on page 27 of this leaflet to indicate your pledge and to have your name flown to Fatima.

Will *YOU Pray*
the ROSARY for Peace?'

Our Lady of Mt. Carmel
Pray for us!

Whosoever dies wearing this Scapular shall not suffer eternal fire.

The Brown Scapular:
A Sign of Our Consecration to Our Lady

In the final vision of Fatima, October 13, 1917, Our Lady held the Brown Scapular from the sky. Sister Lucia said this is because "She wishes everyone to wear it; it is the sign of consecration to Her Immaculate Heart."

The Brown Scapular has been considered from old times in the Church as a sign of the protection of Our Lady. On July 16, 1251, the Blessed Virgin Mary appeared to St. Simon Stock, Superior General of the Carmelite Order. In her hand was a cloth Brown Scapular. She told him: **"Receive the**

15

Brown Scapular. It is a pledge of salvation, a safeguard in danger. Whoever dies wearing this Scapular will never see the flames of hell." Sixty-five years later she revealed her Sabbatine or Saturday privilege to Pope John XXII before he became Pope, that on the first Saturday after their deaths she will free from purgatory all of her scapular children who have fulfilled certain conditions: **"I, the Mother of Graces, shall descend on the Saturday after their deaths, and as many as I find in purgatory I shall free."**

The conditions are: **1) to observe chastity according to one's state in life; 2) to recite the Little Office of the Blessed Virgin Mary daily, or pray five decades of the Rosary. 3) The faithful wearing of the scapular.** The Rosary and the scapular are inseparable!

The word "scapular" is derived from the Latin word "scapula" meaning "shoulder." The Brown Scapular is part of the habit or garment of the priests, brothers, and nuns of the Carmelite Order and it must be worn as they wear it, that is, over the shoulders, with one badge in front and one in back. Thus, when we wear the Brown Scapular we embrace the habit of the Carmelites who have a great devotion to Mary and who have placed themselves under her protection. Pope Pius XII wrote: "For the holy scapular, which may be called the habit or garment of Mary, is a sign and pledge of the protection of the Mother of God." It is as if

Mary is saying "if you wear my habit, faithfully, I will see to it that you never see the fires of hell,"

Pope St. Pius X said, "I wear the cloth, let us never take it off." Sixteen Popes have written about it or indulgenced it. Next to the Rosary it is the most highly indulgenced sacramental in the Church.

Try to wear your brown scapular always, remember that it is a sign of your eternal salvation. If it breaks, tie it or sew it together or purchase a new one. Only a priest or deacon can enroll you in the Brown Scapular. This also enrolls you in the Confraternity of the Blessed Virgin Mary of Mount Carmel which is affiliated to the Carmelite Order and thus you share in all of the daily Masses, prayers, and good works of the members throughout the world. Once you have been officially enrolled, subsequent scapulars do not need to be blessed. The original blessing remains with you for life.

Our Lady's Greatest Gift

Pope Pius XI called the Sabbatine Privilege *"Our greatest privilege from the Mother of God which extends even after death ..."*

This privilege was promulgated by Pope John XXII following an apparition of Our Lady. It promises *freedom from purgatory soon after death,* especially on the first Saturday.

Saints Before We Die

The conditions are simply chastity according to one's state of life, the Scapular, and the Little Office or the Rosary.

This simple formula *will make us saints before we die.* For how could we be freed from Purgatory by the first Saturday after death if we had not by then become holy?

St. Alphonsus, Doctor of the Church, went so far as to say that if we do a little more than this simple formula **"may we not hope that we will not go to Purgatory AT ALL?"**

And forty years after St. Alphonsus' death, his brown scapular was found, midst the corruption of all else in his tomb, perfectly preserved.

Pere Lamy, who saw the coming triumph of the Immaculate Heart of Mary, said: "As for Our Lady, Her kindness gets Her everywhere…A soul that is falling into Hell and calls on Her is helped". *The Blessed Virgin said again to me one day that* **those who have fulfilled the conditions of Her Sabbatine Privilege will be drawn out of Purgatory by Her on the First Saturday after death.**

How Precious!

This was said in 1924, not long after Pope St. Pius X had given permission for the use of the Scapular medal "not excluding the Sabbatine Privilege." (The Pope had given permission for this substitute for the Brown Scapular for serious reason, as used in the trenches during the First World War.) Stressing the importance of the Brown Scapular, Ven. Pere Lamy said:

"How precious then is the Brown Scapular which brings us deliverance from such a place of pain, for Purgatory is extremely painful. The Blessed Virgin told me that it would be better to stay behind 15 years, dragging one's weight on earth, than to spend 15 minutes in Purgatory."

Also, we may remark: How precious is the virtue of chastity! . . . the one virtue which is the prime condition for obtaining this great privilege.

One of the strongest motives for wearing the Scapular (with an understanding that it is an act of faith, hope and love and of consecration to the Immaculate Heart of Mary), is that it is a great aid and safeguard for this beautiful virtue.

How foolish we would be if we were to hesitate even for one moment to put ourselves beneath Our Lady's mantle by being enrolled in Her Scapular! And how foolish again if we would fail to fulfill the other two simple conditions of Her Sabbatine Privilege! . . . *"the greatest of all our privileges from the Mother of God."*

NOTE: The condition of the Sabbatine Privilege that we observe chastity according to our state of life does not mean that if we commit a sin against chastity we will lose the privilege. If we are in the state of Grace and have a sincere intention not to sin, we are fulfilling the Sabbatine condition.

FORMULA OF ENROLLMENT

Priest: Show us, 0 Lord, Thy mercy.
All: And grant us Thy salvation.
Priest: 0 Lord, hear my prayer.
All: And let my cry come unto Thee.
Priest: The Lord be with you.
All: And with your spirit.
Priest: Let us pray:

O Lord Jesus Christ, Savior of mankind, by Thy right hand sanctify † these Scapulars (this Scapular) which Thy servants will devoutly wear for the love of Thee and of Thy mother, the Blessed Virgin Mary of Mount Carmel; so that, by her intercession, they may be protected from the wickedness of the enemy and persevere in Thy grace until death; Who livest and reignest forever and ever.

The priest now sprinkles the Scapular with Holy water, after which he places the Scapular on each one saying:

Priest: Receive this blessed Scapular and ask the Most Holy Virgin that, by her merits, it may be worn with no stain of sin and may protect you from all harm and bring you into everlasting life.

All: Amen.

Priest: By the power granted to me, I admit you to a share in all the spiritual works performed with the merciful help of Jesus Christ, by the Religious of Mount Carmel; in the name of the Father, and of the Son and of the Holy Spirit.

All: Amen.

Priest: May Almighty God, Creator of Heaven and earth, bless † you whom He has been pleased to receive into the Confraternity of the Blessed Virgin Mary of Mount Carmel. We beg her to crush the head of the ancient serpent in the hour of your death, and, in the end, to obtain for you a palm and the crown of your everlasting inheritance. Through Christ Our Lord. Amen.

The priest now sprinkles those enrolled with Holy Water.

Remember, Our Lady of Fatima said:

(These quotations are in the exact order in which Our Lady of Fatima spoke them beginning with the first apparition on May 13, 1917.)

1. **Offering:** "Will you offer yourselves to God and bear with submission all the sufferings He sends you in reparation for the sins that offend Him and the conversion of sinners?"

2. **Blessed Sacrament:** Our Lady opened Her hands and flooded the children in light. They fell to their knees, repeating: Most Holy Trinity, I adore Thee! My God, my God, I love Thee in the Most Blessed Sacrament."

3. **Heaven:** "I come down from heaven." Our Lady promised that the children to whom she appeared would go to heaven, but one of them would have to pray many Rosaries "first."

4. **Purgatory:** "She is in purgatory…" (in reference to a friend, Amelia, who had recently died.)

5. **Rosary:** "Pray the Rosary every day to obtain peace for the world and the end of the war." (In July:) "O my Jesus, forgive us our sins, save us from the fires of hell; lead all souls to heaven, especially those who have most need of Thy mercy."

6. **Immaculate Heart:** "My Immaculate Heart will be your refuge and the way that will lead you to God."

7. **Sacrifices:** "Make sacrifices for sinners and say often, especially when making a sacrifice, "0 Jesus, it is for love of Thee, for the conversion of sinners, and in reparation for the sins committed against the Immaculate Heart of Mary."

8. **Hell:** "You have seen hell, where the souls of poor sinners go. It is to save them that God wants to establish in the world devotion to my Immaculate Heart. If you do what I tell you, many souls will be saved, and there will be peace." Before Our Lady spoke these words, she opened her hands, as Lucia says in her Memoirs, and "we saw a sea of fire. Plunged in this flame were devils and souls that looked like transparent embers; others were black or bronze, and in human form; these were suspended in flames…"

9. **Five Warnings:** "If my requests are not heeded, Russia will spread her errors throughout the world, provoking wars and persecutions of the Church; the good will be martyred, the Holy Father will have much to suffer, and various entire nations will be annihilated."

10. **Peace:** "If my requests are fulfilled, Russia will be converted and there will be peace... Finally, my Immaculate Heart will triumph... an era of peace will be granted to mankind."

11. **Prayer:** "Pray, pray a great deal and make sacrifices for sinners, for many souls go to hell because they have no one to pray and make sacrifices for them."

12. **Amendment of Life:** "I have come to ask the faithful to amend their lives and ask pardon for their sins. They must cease offending God, who is already too much offended!"

13. **St. Joseph:** The only saint who appears at Fatima besides Our Lady, St. Joseph held the Child Jesus in his arms and blessed the people.

14. **Scapular of Mt. Carmel:** In the final vision, on October 13, 1917, Our Lady appeared in the Carmelite habit wearing the Brown Scapular, highlighting the importance of this sacramental.

15. **First Saturday Devotion:** "I promise to assist at the hour of death, with all the graces necessary for salvation, all who on the first Saturday of five consecutive months: 1) Go to Confession; 2) Receive Holy Communion; 3) Pray five decades of the Rosary; and 4) Keep me company for fifteen minutes while mediating on the mysteries of the Rosary; all with the intention of making reparation to my Immaculate Heart."

Before her death, Jacinta revealed the following little-known statements made by Our Lady:

16. **War:** "War is a punishment for sin."
17. **Fashions:** "Certain fashions will be introduced that will offend Our Lord very much."
18. **Matrimony:** "Many marriages are not good, they do not please Our Lord and are not of God."
19. **Priests:** "Priests must be pure, very pure. They should not busy themselves with anything except what concerns the Church and souls. The disobedience of priests to their superiors and to the Holy Father is very displeasing to Our Lord.
20. **Sixth Commandment:** More souls go to hell because of sins of impurity than for any other reason."

My Morning Offering

O my God, in union with the Immaculate Heart of Mary (here kiss your Brown Scapular as a sign of your consecration, partial indulgence also), I offer Thee the Precious Blood of Jesus from all the altars throughout the world, joining with it the offering of my every thought, word and action of this day.

O my Jesus, I desire today to gain every indulgence and merit I can, and I offer them together with myself, to Mary Immaculate—that she may best apply them to the interests of Thy most Sacred Heart. Precious Blood of Jesus, save us! Immaculate Heart of Mary, pray for us! Sacred Heart of Jesus, have mercy on us!

**International Pilgrim Virgin Statue
of Our Lady of Fatima**

I wish to be counted among those who are willing to do the simple things Our Lady asks. Please have my name flown to Fatima.

☐ I have signed the Basic Fatima Pledge. (Pg- 13)

☐ I also offer Our Lady the First Saturday Pledge. (Pg. 14)

Name

_____

Address *(optional)*

_____

_____

NOTE: THESE PLEDGES DO NOT BIND UNDER SIN, BUT EXPRESS A SINCERE INTENTION TO DO WHAT OUR LADY ASKS.

MAIL TO:
INTERNATIONAL PILGRIM VIRGIN
STATUE FOUNDATION, INC.
P.O. BOX 3506
MUNSTER, IN 46321

Fifteen Promises Of The Blessed Virgin To Christians Who Faithfully Pray The Rosary
(Given to Blessed Alan de la Roche)

1. Whosoever shall faithfully serve me by the recitation of the Rosary shall receive signal graces.
2. I promise my special protection and the greatest graces to all those who shall recite the Rosary.
3. The Rosary shall be a powerful armor against hell; it will destroy vice, decrease sin and defeat heresies.
4. It will cause good works to flourish; it will obtain for souls the abundant mercy of God; it will withdraw the hearts of men from the love of the world and its vanities, and will lift them to the desire for Eternal Things. Oh, that souls would sanctify themselves by this means.
5. The soul which recommends itself to me by the recitation of the Rosary shall not perish.
6. Whosoever shall recite the Rosary devoutly, applying himself to the consideration of its Sacred Mysteries shall never be conquered by misfortune. God will not chastise him in His justice, he shall not perish by an unprovided death; if he be just he shall remain in the grace of God, and become worthy of Eternal Life.
7. Whoever shall have a true devotion for the Rosary shall not die without the Sacraments of the Church.
8. Those who are faithful to recite the Rosary shall have during their life and at their death the Light of God and the plenitude of His Graces; at the moment

of death they shall participate in the Merits of the Saints in Paradise.

9. I shall deliver from purgatory those who have been devoted to the Rosary.

10. The faithful children of the Rosary shall merit a high degree of Glory in Heaven.

11. You shall obtain all you ask of me by recitation of the Rosary.

12. All those who propagate the Holy Rosary shall be aided by me in their necessities.

13. I have obtained from my Divine Son that all the advocates of the Rosary shall have for intercessors the entire Celestial Court during their life and at the hour of death.

14. All who recite the Rosary are my Sons, and brothers of my Only Son Jesus Christ.

15. Devotion to my Rosary is a great sign of predestination.